NO REAL LIGHT

NO REAL LIGHT

JOE WENDEROTH

WAVE BOOKS
Seattle • New York

Published by Wave Books
www.wavepoetry.com

Wave Books titles are distributed to the trade by
Consortium Book Sales and Distribution
Phone: 800-283-3572 / SAN 631-760X

Library of Congress Cataloging-in-Publication Data:

Wenderoth, Joe.
  No real light / Joe Wenderoth. — 1st ed.
    p. cm.
  Poems.
ISBN 978-1-933517-23-0 (limited edition hardcover : alk. paper) —
ISBN 978-1-933517-22-3 (trade paper : alk. paper)
  I. Title.
  PS3573.E515N6 2007
  811'.54—dc22

  2007012346

Designed and composed by J. Johnson
Printed in the United States of America

9 8 7 6 5 4 3 2 1

First Edition

Wave Books 011

Contents

The Weight Of What Is Thrown

Smooth stones have always appealed to me.
River stones, I guess they're called,
though the best ones come from ocean shoreline
where cliffs are crumbling and tides are rising
and falling
and perfecting what they have broken.
In Maine, for instance,
there are beaches of big smooth stones—
the stones are piled deep
like those plastic balls in a kids' carnival attraction.
And each night, and each morning,
in comes the weight of the water,
the weight of the ocean,
under which the stones turn on one another
until they are smooth,
until they demonstrate submission to a kind of rule—
we might call it *the rule*
of the weight of what is thrown.
The stones are smooth like eggs, sometimes,
or like a palette;
whatever shape they are,
they are evidence of the rule,
evidence of the always diminishing shape of origin.
This is what we mean by *decorative.*

I say like an egg, but what a strange egg.
Think of a creature of bone—entirely of bone.
Such creatures are not born;

such creatures are *made.*
I suppose it's appealing to suggest that something other
than human artifice could be a maker.
That is, it's satisfying to think
that the weight of the ocean
and the weight of meaning
could be in some way connected.
Perhaps we can't help but to explore that fantasy.

A smooth stone, like a word,
is artificially refined.
Pick it out of its bed
and take it up into your grasp
and it is strange.
Why is it strange?
It is strange because it is so *telling*—
because, like a corpse, it so plainly confronts us
with its nonsensical independence.
How could the earth be a heap of smooth stones?
How could speech be a heap of words?
But unlike a corpse, it's appealing
to take a smooth stone to hand.
A smooth stone is a weapon, and,
assuming it's the right size, an attractive weapon.
It's a weapon, moreover, that promises a great event.
The event is great because it alludes to
and calls for a certain talent,
a certain potential in its thrower.

A language, at any given moment, is so many words.
It's one beach, let's say, along a world-ocean.
I think of the way they named the portions of beach
on D-Day: *Juno, Sword, Omaha, Utah, Gold.*
Expand that map and you can picture
all the earth's language-beaches.
Some are so close to one another that they overlap—
others are quite far apart.
No matter how far apart, however,
their differences are superficial.
Each beach is smooth stones,
and the stones have not been born—
they have been made.
Not made like a bicycle, mind you—
not made *intentionally*—
but made by weight,
made by a great thrown force,
thrown by No One, really,
for who-knows-what reason.
Perhaps this is why, when someone hurls words at us
like they are his own,
like the weight of the words is his own weight,
we are so mistrustful, so appalled.

Only the voice of No One
is really moving.

All There Is

the bliss of the lure
fully erect

(brain damage)

dumb with hope
dumb with hope

Preference

I like to see penetration.
Sun in the trees.
Sun in the grass.
Deep grave
in the names
we call,
deep halt
in the laughter
that got us here.

Physis

If we knew what we were up against,
the slept-in room would still ache
from the dreamt word—
    the breathlessness—
in every siren's unmeant distance.

Luck

So a screaming woke you
just in time.
An animal's scream, or animals'.
What kind of animal it was
doesn't matter, and cannot,
in any case, be determined.
The point is you are saved.
Your mouth has been opened.

Regarding The Intentional Attendance Of Poetry Readings

Our neighbors, directly behind us,
have an aviary. Maybe eighty birds:
cockatiels, parrots, parakeets,
little tropical songbirds.
Sometimes a sparrow hawk,
a native to the region,
comes and sits on top of the cage.
I've seen him,
seen the way he comes.
The racket beneath him, curiously enough,
doesn't surge,
doesn't die down.
The racket, it seems, doesn't know any better—
the racket is forever the racket.
He sits atop it,
conspicuous in his silence,
alien,
barely bothering to look down
through the screen.
What his sitting there means to accomplish
can
in rare pressing lulls
be distinguished from happy departure.

Costume

I find myself sometimes, evening,
in a strange costume,
a costume from some forgotten regime.
No one is looking.
I'm driving to the stores,
singing.
My voice is all imitation soft,
decay upon decay. .

This evening is distant applause.
Decay upon decay.

Read This First

The bride is of the air,
laid out like a sharp knife in the tall grass—
take away the light and make the sound.
The vow is of that knife, rusted in years
of heavy rain—lock the doors
and you're not there:
the groom,
the made sound.

Letter Home

I took a pin to my eyes
broke the surface tension
and scooped out the machinery
useless there beneath

I sewed shut the lids
singing
myself to sleep

I watched the sun rise
with my skin and my brain

while my bloody pin
began guardedly to speak

Operation Enduring Freedom

like an eagle
into the sun

over frozen fields

bone-fed grasses

Where I Lie

When I wake to piss, it's late,
and Romana is still downstairs, cooking.
It's oddly quiet, the TV not on.
Back in bed, I remember
that I should take Annika in.
She's four, still sleeps in our bed,
and still has accidents sometimes.
She's sound asleep in my arms
as I carry her down the hall.
I stand her up in front of the toilet;
her bare feet on the cold floor
half-wake her.
When she has gone,
I send her stumbling back into the darkness.
She's back to sleep in seconds.
    I look at her there, touch her face.
And I ask myself the same old question:
would it have been better
    to have never been born,
to have never come into the need
to lose this face?

The house is quiet.
The less and less possible surge
of yes and no at the same time
is where I lie.

Ex-Lover Somewhere

now to me your face is a flower
   on film
moving from full bloom to seed
in high-speed slow-motion
(we've all seen this in school)
each frame retracting
   shape   color
until the silent unreal dominance
of the film
resumes
its having never

Brutal Recluse

I've always wanted to be exposed.
Very early on I came to sense
it was just me that ate away
the on-going summer surface,
all the faces and their never breathing.
I've always wanted to be strapped down
there
in summer's dumb-lit shallows,
a blind warm thrash
in the way the words for it
are buried alive
and bound to feed forever.

Octopus

Of all creatures you are closest to human.
You walk along the deep bottom,
which you love,
which you mirror, continually,
appearance and hunger
intertwined in billions of nerves.
You have no hard parts,
save your mouth.
You do not speak.
You carry ink,
for others as much as for yourself.
For the distinction between the two.
You know well the narrow places.
You reserve countenance for the moment
from which you cannot flee.
Your final talent, in that moment,
is to appear
as nothing recognizable.
And that is what,
in your short dark life,
sometimes saves you.

What Does Death Insure

death insures
that one will never hear
again
the sound of a small plane
sketched out in the sand
of a windless summer afternoon

Narrative Poem

Gradually I got to aching so bad
that I couldn't lie still.
I had a fever every day for a few years.
I took out school loans.
I watched a little TV in a little room.
I took pills.
I moved my pills and my little TV from city to city,
watching with delight, with loathing.
The ache withdrew, at long last,
into the foundation,
lapping more softly at the bones.
My lover and I drove to Canada
and bought codeine.
We watched a TV movie
in a resort motel in the off-season.
We drove back and rented a house in Baltimore.
We got credit.
We bought a 32-inch TV and a new couch—
two thousand dollars, all told.
I kicked out the driver's side window of our car
in a Denny's parking lot.
I filed an insurance claim;
valuable objects had been taken from the car.
We ran out of codeine.
I couldn't afford to get the window fixed.
We drove all winter with the window down.
Our neighbor gave us an old aquarium

and I bought two piranha.
I feed them a goldfish every morning.
Sometimes one will get its head and its tail torn off;
even so, it swims around the tank awhile.

Eurydice's Complaint

Why carry on with this hellish trek?
Look at me already.
Look!
Let them come already
and cut you into the strange brevity
of a wedding day.
I am not with you—
I do not follow—
except that you acknowledge
my sudden silent burial,
except that you are torn apart
where I am already gone.

Wedding Vow

—for Kevin and Britney

cleave you
unto this here
promise of nothing
but

whither you might lodge
brained singing
in the eat
of a brief mount

Word

We'll begin with what's irreplaceable.
If you have one photograph, for instance,
of someone you loved,
someone who's gone now—
we'll begin with that.
Put it in the fire.
Isn't it like felling
—at once—
a whole herd?
When the dust has settled,
you feel like you should say a few words, don't you?
All the words
begin to fall
and you will not live
to hear their dust
settled.

Advice To The Dissertator

Quit the brilliant dream plot and stand on knives
until all the god-costumes have been lost
and hang in Museums.
Exercise, then, upon the Museum Grounds,
knowing more or less what hangs inside
and why.

Academia

To pimp the fine young cadence
of the dying gasp's demented urge
to sentence
                              and to dumb back the ecstasies
that press up from, well, NOTHING—
this is our tiny calling,
our bungled ancientness.

For My Brother

Your soul is a million dollars cash
and you're playing blackjack
five dollars a hand.
Very hard to stay interested, some nights.
Harder still, in these long afternoons,
to conceive of how to raise the stakes.
You learn, of course, in time,
how foolish it is to want that raise;
you have not come to the table, after all,
to win—you've come to lose.
It's best, then, that the blind sweep
preceding decision means this little,
and seems this vulnerable to the grim intelligence
we cannot help but to call our own.
There is certainly pleasure in the bizarre hours
of freedom from intelligence—
the drunken fuck of seeming on the verge
of destroying the house utterly—
and there's pleasure, too, in seeing others
in this light: giddy bodies come suddenly
into the hope that they'll take everything
and walk out—just walk out into real light
with everything.
But freedom from intelligence is overrated,
ultimately, and it is weakness, not strength,
that proposes we could ever walk away
from our hands, or from knowing the odds

against which our gestures make sense.
Sense, which is really only time.
Time for what?
Time to celebrate, time to grieve.
Time for the luxurious darkness of the house,
which your gestures have never touched,
and which your intelligence has never brightened,
and which your soul, steadily clarified by loss,
has never stopped calling home.

Walt Whitman

sense
     imposed
might have become fettered
the instrument
of a privileged language
   but in you
a portion of our deplorable amount
burned
       the victory
   the defeat
 forever

founded
   extraordinary null matter
   and as such
punishable by writing   *Death*
   I declare   *for opposing this*
herewith quashed   *decree*
   all persons
immediately set at liberty
   restored
     anyone

*

up
abolished
    prayers continue
in the exercise of the petty states
    once more
                    for none
sought

*

when it fell
    the order of things
actually issued
    and industry
and false steps were taken
            think of destroying all that

*

I derive   always
interested spectators
for the purpose of oppressing them
    in any other light

*

anything mechanical
    (either in theory or in practice)
        will guess my astonishment
the torture
    is saturated
by plumb luck

*

a vulgar use of the eye
receives the entire pattern
almost in the same moment
     the saving of labor   is immense
and is actually capable
of the striking facts
     machinery has constantly
to be devised
to make machinery
until there seems to be no end to the
acute observer

*

in order to produce a given word
hold and guide   the sound
     become useless
     a cheap reproduction
          of long hours

*

there was the sound
there was
but the country never saw

Stevens Walked To Work

life is move-
ment meant

        woe to mo-
mentum

        woe
to him

      what
don't move

Aside

I've stopped breathing on occasion.
There's room,
after all.

You don't simply tell someone.

Regarding Venus

I.

> We lose sight
> of how beautiful
> it is
> that it is captured,
> and kept,
> open-lipped
> in the dominant recess.

II.

> I watch you move,
> without words,
> for an hour.
> When it's done
> you speak right into me
> and laugh,
> and your laughter
> is a naked marching band
> in dense dark woods.

Privacy

I hope all the Jacksons live to old age.
I hope in old age they all get together—
in Indonesia, let's say—
to have a picture taken.
Michael, La Toya, Janet, Jermaine,
and all the rest,
in whatever's left of their fineries,
smiling,
remembering nothing
so much
as the ridiculous hope
of the opened shutter.

Light The Arrows

a baby
(wearing just a diaper)
crawls up onto an elephant's head
crawls up toward the trunk

a second baby
slightly smaller than the first
(wearing just a diaper)
rides the first baby
like a man would ride a very small horse

only there are no reins
so the riding baby has to hold on
to the crawling baby's hair

when they reach the top of the elephant's skull
and begin to move down toward the trunk
        the weight of their heads
becomes more difficult for them to control

fortunately
the elephant is surrounded by gifted archers
who light their arrows
and draw their bows
in anticipation of the unimaginable
loss of context

I-90

posture
is continually
at issue

open your face then
and take it

be as blind as the drive
is

stand down
and get sung up
from the missing wreck

Recognition

When I got home from work at the Kwik Trip
it was 7:30 or so.
I warmed up some cabbage,
took some codeine and turned on the TV.
Sated, I went out back and built a fire in the fire-pit.
Wet wood, dusk, sixty-some degrees
and getting cooler by the minute.
Put on the porch-light so I could read.
I read *The Dream Songs,*
sitting by the fire.
Attention waxing and waning.
Something popping in one of the boards
in the fire. Sparks dying
in the black grass, and the porch-light
still trying to make it green.
Brought my tape-player out
and put in Loretta Lynn.
Got a can of beer and drank it,
looking into the fire.
I tended the fire, which was getting hot,
less smoke, but still popping.
I felt good, I thought.
Something to do with the codeine coming on,
the beer in the cold can,
the escalating heat of the fire,
and the beautiful song in the dark air.
I stopped reading.

Started listening to the music
and looking harder into the fire.
The tape ended.
I thought about all my past lovers,
that strange progression of ghosts.
I thought
it would be good to sit with them here,
by this fire,
to hear their voices again,
and to force recognition to come
to this ultra-dim place,
these too-bright inflections.

Miles

my dream feeds on me
like a school of small fish
feeds on
a sinking stone

Moon River

what is true
is what seems the most

to repeat location
without mercy

the blank bark of old animals
the house
the way the snow has not shifted

the few songs that seem again
to have stayed

Sitting In Traffic

These days I often see those yellow-ribbon bumper stickers.
Support Our Troops,
or *God Bless America,*
they intoned, once,
but now they're all faded
and it's hard to make out the words.
When you can't make out the words,
you notice the transparent plastic strip—
its tenacious adhesive—
and the rubber or the steel
that will go on making a way
where there really is none,
transparency after transparency
adorning whatever it is that moves us
no closer to knowing.

God's Plan

First you are caused to careen and/or stagger
through situations of indescribable appeal
and mind-breaking vertiginous sadness.
Then you are smothered.

Home-Owner's To-Do List

- Organize toys according to imagined sound
- Dust the hammer at each peep-hole
- Sterilize the peripheral troughs
- Cut grass
- Dig the mine deeper
- Sprinkle blood around the yard

King Hiram

there is
           where this all rings true

no real light

Coltrane

borne deaf
upon rhythmic kill-all

face down
eyes open

what sounds
like it matters
is—
the pull of the current—
is always
what you can't see

Against Zoning

in my mind it's full nude all the time
and never the same dancers

Twentieth-Century Pleasures

A woman has two children:
one is seven, a girl with Down syndrome,
and one is five, a deaf-mute boy.
Every day, the woman's husband beats her
and calls her a lazy whore.
After a few years
the woman moves back into her mother's house.
She locks the doors when her mother is at work,
but her husband, having promised to kill her,
gets in through a basement window.
When she hears and meets him in the basement,
pleading for her life,
he breaks her spine with a hammer.
As the two children watch from the steps,
he shoots her in the back of the head,
then turns the gun on himself.
The seven-year old, the girl with Down syndrome,
runs four blocks to the police station.
When the police arrive at the house,
the five-year old,
the poet,
a deaf-mute boy,
is kneeling by his mother's head,
pressing the pool of blood back toward her.
They pull him away and he doesn't resist.
They think he has been playing there
in a pool of his mother's blood.

That is truly what they think:
he was playing in a pool of his dead mother's blood.
Later, with his bloody hands
he says things they cannot understand,
and they know then, at least,
that he was not playing.

Sitcom

Say the sun was born at 6 a.m.
and will die at 6 p.m.
It is now 10:36 a.m.
Late morning.
Our species has been around
for less than one second.
In four minutes, at 10:40 a.m.,
it will be too hot to live on earth.
The sun is getting hotter.
The sun is an explosion.
We survive via proximity to an explosion
that is getting hotter.

Evening With Shows

Less now,
by these pretended wounds
I go at it,
by these little bits
I stay at home.

Less now,
with more at a time,
lit up,
turned down,
able to breathe.

Less now,
bundled down
into rapid gazes,
cleaned up
with gorgeous shadow,
I have only
not to hold
this.

Asleep In Steerage

the hideous music
that feeds the stems

(break and rot and never dream)
(break and rot and never dream)

I sew my tent into the water
as the captives are slain

(break and rot and never dream)
(break and rot and never dream)

I sew my tent into the water
as the free are taken captive

(break and rot and never dream)
(break and rot and never dream)

the hideous music
that feeds the stems

The Home Of The Brave

—after the Nick Berg decapitation video

The home of the brave is a small room.
At first, it mimics us.
Armed men stand side by side.
They are aware of their power.
They have concealed their identities.
Only their leader speaks,
and he speaks at length,
reading from a prepared statement,
foregrounding their intentions
with weak rhetoric,
belief in God.
His comrades fidget and remain silent.
When the screaming begins,
the camera shakes
with a new honesty—
mimicry is done with now—
the men bear down,
and the home of the brave
is what we cannot understand,
what we cannot endure,
so long as we are free.

In The Führer-Bunker

—for W.

Decency reigns.
Meals come on time.
A great city, in miniature,
has been laid out,
and is dreamt upon.
This is the city of tomorrow.

At The AWP Hotel Bar

No one remains: *a priori.* —Derrida

Even so . . .
some agony aunts do seem
to stagger out.

Let them all be stacked.

Vacation Vow

what there will be
between us

it alone
it alone

exotic enough
to inform
our always
having simply
not known

Burglar Fondles Sleeping Resident

mental illness
broken feet
metastasis
    these seizures of fate
are nothing like breath
nothing like breathing
and it has always come to this
the way someone is beaten to death
the way I see you
fall in love
can't breathe
and can't leave
with anything of value

Craft

song
is the thirst of the decided
how the gone moan and coo at the blood
the night river carries always this close
to that shore

poem
is how the going
the live crew
deny their own blood
struggling in silence with their impossible craft
as it drifts them in almost too close
to the endless distress
of shadow

Fame

stars cohere you
with stone
deaf might

listen

you can't
in your own mind
decide

College

I remember I had a plastic cup
with too much bourbon and not enough ice
and I was tripping a little bit too hard . . .
and so I thought I had better try to *say* something,
try to get a ride home,
or find a door I could lock.
It was at this point,
or perhaps one moment beyond this point,
that the spotlight hit me—
and I was center stage,
and I was *no one*—
I was not a part of the production on any level.
I froze.
I felt the dumb luck of my face
withstanding the delicate silence
of an audience that can't be acted out
and can't be made to understand
that this is not an act.

Troll Inn

gouging the casual quiet vow
of roadhouse shadows

a good dream idles
in the dying business of the late hour

idles
that is
in the regular shameful wish
to admit more than it has ever had

the sense

to carry out

Regarding Your Last Words

take not light
but the small roar
at the base of light

take the easy breath
in which that roar grew up

take as much as you can imagine taking
and hide what you've taken in the words
you have now to speak

there may be live darkness
enough to see you in
after all

At The Races

never quite buried altogether
       you and I
in summer's
newer-than-new
same light

groom the dumb
breath-taking
throng of sprints

resigned again
to put everything we have
on the animal
that never comes in

Mother Of God

this many years
you have poured the darkness over me
and still I do not shine

Where I Stand With Regard To The Game

At first, I played the game
as I was given to play the game.
I played without grace, without pretense—
I played with pure joy, and with a brutality all my own.
I played the game without understanding
that there was a game.
This could not continue.
I could not help but to be taken in by the others,
by the warmth of their casual concern.
I had a great potential for grace, they said,
so I gave myself to them.
I learned how to hold a pretense,
how to hold myself in check,
and in my play there gradually arose
a kind of grace, a swift intelligence about the game.
This could not continue.
Pretense gave rise to grace, I gathered,
and so I held myself even more firmly in check.
I withdrew as powerfully as I had at first played.
The game went on around me
and I taught myself to keep out of it—
I taught myself to watch.
To demonstrate my decided detachment,
I began to describe the game.
At first, the lay of the field,
the way the weather came,
and how the light made the mood

in which the players were given to play.
Then I described the players themselves,
the waxing and waning of their graces,
and the shouts that seemed to be the glory
of certain residency, or certain vacancy.
The shouts, that is, that defied description.
I turned away from them—
turned away from my failure to describe them—
turned instead to the rules of the game,
which everyone had to admit
had never really been clarified.
How is the field of play bounded,
and how is this binding productive of zones within itself?
And the techniques the players make use of—
what is legal and what is not?
How should the children,
who soon enough will begin to play,
move out onto the field?
There was room here for wisdom such as mine
to make itself known—to make fresh remarks.
In clarifying the rules of the game,
I no longer felt graceful, exactly,
but I did feel as though I was developing a clarity
in which the graces of the extant players
would have to be more apparent—
more accessible, if you will.
I also felt that, so long as I was clarifying
the rules of the game, I could not be blamed

for my failure to describe the shouts of the players.
As I worked, the game went on, of course,
untouched by my efforts.
As I poured forth my eloquent logics
and settled fine points never before addressed,
it was as though the players were not listening.
I felt, at first, that this was not of any consequence—
the players, in the midst of play,
could not reasonably be expected to listen to me.
I realized, however, as time went by,
and as my work became
an increasingly undeniable success,
that even those who were *not* playing,
those who, like myself, were content to watch—
even *those* were not at all interested
in making the amendments to the rules
that my hard and subtle work made prescient.
This irked me.
I began to ask myself why I continued with my work.
I began to write less about the rules of the game
and more about why I felt the need to clarify said rules.
The question of play arose—
the question, that is, of whether or not
I should have ever *stopped* playing,
and the question of whether or not
it would be possible to resume play,
to play *now*.
I began to speculate, from the incredible distance

I had worked years to create,
about the potential benefits of a life of play.
Such speculation only proved the distance
I had worked so many years to create.
If I was to resume play—
if I was to abandon everything I had ever worked for
in favor of again embracing a life of play—
there could be no graceful approach.
There could be no speculation.
There would have to be something new,
something defying description.
There would have to be
a complete and hopeless destruction
of every grace, every distance.
And that is where I stand.

Notes

Home-Owner's To-Do List: I dedicate this poem to Ben Marcus.

Twentieth-Century Pleasures: The story in this poem is, more or less verbatim, a story I heard told on a daytime talk show—I can't recall which one. It was alleged to be a true story. The show's topic may have been domestic violence.

Regarding Venus: The poem's impetus was my being asked to write about the beauty of Venus Williams.

What Does Death Insure: This poem seems somehow indebted to the work of Sherwood Anderson.

Troll Inn: I dedicate this poem to Tweety, bartender at the Troll Inn in Mt. Horeb, Wisconsin.

King Hiram: This poem is indebted to Hank Williams.

———

Joe Wenderoth's work can be seen on YouTube.

Acknowledgments

Thanks to Romana Norton, Francisco Reinking,
Greg Miller, Mark Peacock Brush, Matthew Zapruder,
and anyone else who helped me with these poems.